THE REAL
Alexander Graham Bell

Virginia Loh-Hagan

45th Parallel Press

Published in the United States of America by Cherry Lake Publishing
Ann Arbor, Michigan
www.cherrylakepublishing.com

Reading Adviser: Marla Conn MS, Ed., Literacy specialist, Read-Ability, Inc.
Book Cover Design: Felicia Macheske

Photo Credits: © Library of Congress/Harris & Ewing [Between 1905 and 1945]/Reproduction
No. LC-DIG-hec-15690, Cover, 1; © Bruno Passigatti/Shutterstock.com, Cover, 1; © Everett Historical/
Shutterstock.com, 5, 7, 27, 29; © Elzbieta Sekowska/Shutterstock.com, 9; © Library of Congress/
Reproduction No. LC-G9-Z4-116,794-T, 11, 30; © Andrey_Popov/Shutterstock.com, 12; © Valentin Georgiev/
Shutterstock.com, 15; © Johanna Altmann/Shutterstock.com, 17; © Library of Congress/Underwood &
Underwood [1915-1925]/Reproduction No. LC-DIG-det-4a27975, 19; © Fer Gregory/Shutterstock.com, 20;
© Library of Congress/Carl Mydans [1936]/Reproduction No. LC-USF33-T01-000381-M4, 23; © The New York
Public Library Digital Collections/Verelst, John & Simon, John [1657-1890], 24

Graphic Elements Throughout: © iulias/Shutterstock.com; © Thinglass/Shutterstock.com;
© kzww/Shutterstock.com; © A_Lesik/Shutterstock.com; © MegaShabanov/Shutterstock.com;
© Groundback Atelier/Shutterstock.com; © saki80/Shutterstock.com

45th Parallel Press is an imprint of Cherry Lake Publishing.

Library of Congress Cataloging-in-Publication Data

Names: Loh-Hagan, Virginia, author.
Title: The real Alexander Graham Bell / by Virginia Loh-Hagan.
Description: Ann Arbor : Cherry Lake Publishing, [2019] | Series: History uncut |
    Includes bibliographical references and index.
Identifiers: LCCN 2018035188 | ISBN 9781534143333 (hardcover) | ISBN 9781534141094 (pdf) |
    ISBN 9781534139893 (pbk.) | ISBN 9781534142299 (hosted ebook)
Subjects: LCSH: Bell, Alexander Graham, 1847-1922—Juvenile literature. |
    Inventors—United States—Biography—Juvenile literature.
Classification: LCC TK6143.B4 L64 2019 | DDC 621.385092 [B]—dc23
LC record available at https://lccn.loc.gov/2018035188

Cherry Lake Publishing would like to acknowledge the work of The Partnership for 21st Century Skills.
Please visit www.p21.org for more information.

Printed in the United States of America
Corporate Graphics

Table of Contents

Chapter 1
Alexander Graham Bell
The Story You Know 4

Chapter 2
An Odd Birthday Present 6

Chapter 3
Mama's Boy 10

Chapter 4
Piano Player 14

Chapter 5
Bell's Talking Dog 18

Chapter 6
Bad Student, Good Teacher, Great Inventor 22

Chapter 7
Honoring an Inventive Life 26

Timeline 30

Consider This! 31
Learn More 31
Glossary 32
Index 32
About the Author 32

Alexander Graham Bell
The Story You Know

Alexander Graham Bell did much for the deaf community. Deaf means not being able to hear. Bell was an inventor. He had almost 20 patents. Patents are special ownership rights. Bell is most famous for inventing the telephone.

He worked with Thomas Watson. Watson was a skilled electrician. Bell came up with the ideas. Watson brought those ideas to life. In 1876, magic happened. Bell said, "Mr. Watson. Come here. I want you!" Watson heard it over the wires. This was the first telephone call.

Bell's work changed people's lives. He paved the way for technology. But there is more to his story …

Bell founded the Bell Telephone Company in 1877.

CHAPTER 2

An Odd Birthday Present

Bell was born on March 3, 1847. He was born in Scotland. His father was Alexander Melville Bell. He was a professor. He studied and taught the sounds of human speech. Bell's mother was Eliza Grace Bell. Bell had two brothers. One was named Edward Charles Bell. Another was named Melville James Bell. Both brothers got sick. Edward died in 1867. Melville died 3 years later.

Bell was born without a middle name. He was simply Alexander Bell. He wanted a middle name. He was named after his father and grandfather. Both were named Alexander. Bell wanted a middle name to be different from them.

Bell's father, grandfather, and uncle all worked
in the speech and hearing field.

SETTING THE WORLD STAGE
1847

- The Treaty of Cahuenga was signed. This ended the Mexican-American War in California. It was an informal agreement between military forces. Both sides gave up their weapons. They freed their prisoners. The treaty was signed at Campo de Cahuenga. Today, this is North Hollywood in Los Angeles.

- The U.S. Post Office issued its first postage stamps. One stamp was 5 cents. It honored Benjamin Franklin. Another stamp was 10 cents. It honored George Washington.

- The Zenkoji earthquake happened in Japan. It killed about 9,000 people. It destroyed 34,000 homes and temples.

- Liberia is a country in Africa. It was declared an independent nation. It modeled its government after the United States. Liberia's capital is Monrovia. It was named after James Monroe. Monroe was the fifth U.S. president.

"Before anything else, preparation is the key to success." — Alexander Graham Bell

At age 10, he begged his father to give him a middle name. He begged and begged. He wore his father down. For his 11th birthday, Bell got his wish. He was allowed to take the name Graham. The name was chosen to honor Alexander Graham. Graham was a close family friend.

Bell liked the sound of "Alexander Graham Bell." But his family called him Aleck. Years later, when he got married, his wife asked him to spell it "Alec." After that, he signed his name "Alec Bell."

He gave his daughters middle names. Their names were Elsie May Bell and Marian Hubbard Bell. His two sons died when they were babies.

Bell was the only one of his brothers who didn't have a middle name.

CHAPTER 3

Mama's Boy

Bell had two very important women in his life. His mother was one. The other was his wife, Mabel Hubbard Bell. They both were deaf. They inspired Bell's work.

Bell was very close to his mother. He spent a lot of time with her. Eliza was his first teacher. She taught him to be curious about the world. She became deaf when Bell was 12 years old. She made her own hearing aid. It was a tube. The tube connected to her ear to whatever she wanted to hear. Bell spoke into the tube when he talked to his mother. He thought there was a better way.

Bell had two sons and two daughters.
Only his daughters lived to be adults.

He put his lips on her forehead. He spoke in clear tones. Eliza felt his breath. She felt the **vibrations** of his voice. Vibrations are moving sound waves. Eliza could understand him.

But she still couldn't hear at parties. So Bell came up with another idea. He was inspired by his father's work. His father invented visible speech. Visible means easily seen. Bell used a **manual** alphabet. Manual means by hand. He sat next to Eliza. He spelled words with his fingers. He tapped them out. He did this on Eliza's palms, fingers, and knuckles. He was able to include her in conversations this way. Eliza's deafness led Bell to study sounds.

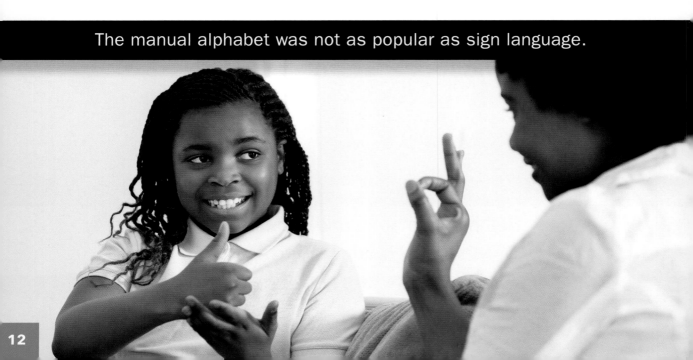

The manual alphabet was not as popular as sign language.

All in the Family

Mabel Hubbard Bell was Bell's wife. She got scarlet fever at age 5. She lost her hearing. She could read lips in several languages. She was Bell's student at age 15. She married Bell at age 20. She was the first woman to invest in the aviation business. Aviation means flight. She did this in 1907. She formed and managed the Aerial Experiment Association. This was a flight company. Two years later, her group launched the Silver Dart. This was a small plane. It was the first human flight in Canada. Bell did a lot for the community. She supported women. She founded Canada's first and longest-running women's club. She founded a parent-teacher group. She founded Canada's first Montessori school. She founded a library. She died 5 months after Bell. On her husband's desk, he kept a picture of his wife. He wrote on the back, "The girl for whom the telephone was invented."

"Sometimes we stare so long at a door that is closing that we see too late the one that is open." — Alexander Graham Bell

CHAPTER 4

Piano Player

Bell's mother was an excellent pianist. She placed one end of her ear tube on the piano. She placed the other end in her ear. She taught Bell how to play. She said he had "musical fever."

Bell had a gift for playing the piano. He quickly learned to read music. He also played by ear. He could play songs by just listening to them.

His mother got him the best piano teacher in town. His name was Auguste Benoit Bertini. Bertini wanted Bell to be a professional pianist. So did Bell. But then Bertini died. Bell lost interest in playing professionally. But he played piano his whole life.

Bell became the family pianist.

THAT
Happened?!?

Bell helped create a new job for women. Everyone was using the telephone. This required a telephone exchange system. There was a switchboard between callers. Callers picked up the phone. They spoke with operators. Operators connected them to other people. Edward Holmes owned a switchboard company. He hired teenage boys. This was a big mistake. The boys messed around. They were rude. They said bad words. Holmes realized boys were bad for business. He said, "Why not have girls?" Bell sold phones to Holmes. He told Holmes to hire Emma Nutt. Nutt became the first female telephone operator. Stella Nutt was her sister. She was hired a few hours later. She became the second female telephone operator. The Nutt sisters were patient. They were polite. They had calming voices. They were better workers. Other companies copied Holmes. Soon, women took over the operator business.

"Great discoveries and improvements invariably involve the cooperation of many minds." — Alexander Graham Bell

Bell said, "My early love of music had a good deal to do in preparing me for the scientific study of sound." Playing piano made him an expert listener. Bell could hear small differences in **pitch**. Pitch is the quality of sound. It can be high or low.

Bell studied his piano. A piano note in one room can be copied by a piano in another room. Bell realized sounds travel in the air. They vibrated at exactly the same pitch. This gave him the idea of sending messages at different pitches across wires.

Bell was creative in other ways. He wrote poems. He did art. He did voice tricks.

When they were younger, Bell and his brothers put on puppet shows.

CHAPTER 5

Bell's Talking Dog

When Bell was 16 years old, his father took him to see an **automaton**. Automatons are moving machines. They're made to copy humans. They're like robots.

This inspired Bell. Bell read about automatons. He and his brothers tried to make their own. They made it look lifelike. They made it say a few words.

Bell continued to **experiment**. Experiment means to test. It also means to play around. When Bell was 20 years old, he used the family dog. Trouve was a Skye terrier. He was a hunting dog. He had long hair. He liked treats. Bell gave him treats to do his bidding.

The Detroit News Timely Topics

Bell's First Telephone

UNDERWOOD & U
WASHI

Bell created speaking machines.

Bell taught the dog to growl for a long time. Then, he grabbed the dog's mouth. He moved the dog's lips. He moved the dog's throat. He made the dog utter different sounds. The dog said, "Ow ah oo ga ma ma." It sounded like, "How are you, Grandmama?" People thought Bell had a talking dog.

Bell also experimented with a human ear. He needed a human ear to test sound waves. His invention could help deaf people "see" the sound of words. Bell asked medical schools for a human ear. He got one in the mail. The ear came from a dead person's body. Bell used the ear to track sound patterns.

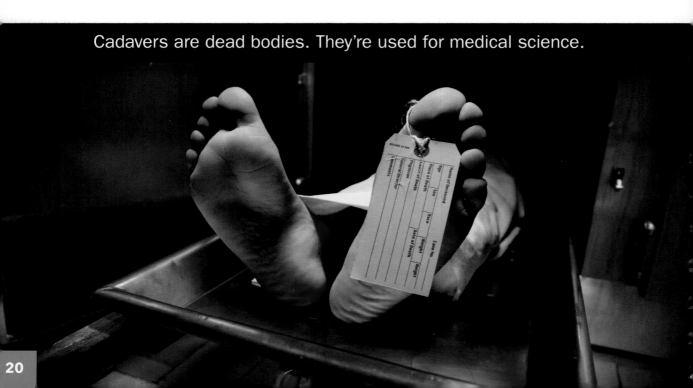

Cadavers are dead bodies. They're used for medical science.

Bad Blood

Elisha Gray lived from 1835 to 1901. He was an American inventor. He was an electrical engineer. He competed with Bell. Gray and Bell had a famous legal battle. Legal means of the law. Gray and Bell went to court several times. They fought over who invented the telephone first. Some people think Gray invented the telephone. They think Bell stole his idea. Gray founded the Western Electric Company. He announced his intention to file a patent for the telephone. He did this on the same day as Bell. But Bell beat him. The courts gave Bell the patent. Gray was upset. He sold his invention to a company. This company competed with Bell's company. Bell's company sued. The companies came to an agreement. Gray didn't quit. He became a college professor. He got 70 other patents. He helped invent fax machines. He worked on underwater signaling devices.

"The only difference between success and failure is the ability to take action." — Alexander Graham Bell

CHAPTER 6

Bad Student, Good Teacher, Great Inventor

Bell wasn't the best student. He went to school in Scotland. He left at age 15. He skipped classes a lot. He got bad grades. But he loved science. He was also good at solving problems. At age 12, he noticed how slow the process of cleaning wheat grain was. It was normally done by hand. So, he invented a machine to do this work. Bell only focused on learning things he liked. This made his father mad.

Bell was sent to London. He lived with his grandfather. He started to love school. At age 16, he became a teacher. He taught speech and music. He learned Greek and Latin.

In his early years, Bell was taught by his parents.

He moved to Canada at age 23 and then the United States. He set up a "dreaming place." This was his workshop. He continued to study sounds. He trained teachers at several schools for the deaf. He taught at schools for the deaf in Massachusetts, Connecticut, and London. In 1872, Bell started his own school. He believed he could teach deaf people to speak. He didn't support learning sign language. He wanted deaf people to live like most people.

Bell gave up teaching in 1873. He wanted to spend more time inventing. He had many inventions. He invented a metal jacket to help with breathing. He invented a machine to find icebergs. He invented a fast speedboat. He invented special kites.

◀ Bell learned a Native American language.

CHAPTER 7

Honoring an Inventive Life

President James Garfield was shot. This happened on July 2, 1881. Doctors kept poking at his body. They used dirty fingers. They used dirty tools. They were trying to find the bullet.

Bell said, "Science should be able to discover some less **barbarous** method" for finding the bullet. Barbarous means cruel. Bell created a special machine. His machine was like a metal detector.

Bell went to the White House twice. His machine didn't find bullets. There were steel wires on the bed. These wires confused the machine. Also, the bullet was lodged too deeply. The president died.

Bell tested his machine on Civil War veterans.
Veterans are soldiers who fought in wars.

SCIENCE

Sound travels to the brain. Sound waves reach the outer ear. Then, these waves move down the ear path to the eardrum. They cause the eardrum to vibrate. These vibrations then move through three tiny ear bones. These ear bones are in the middle ear. This transfers the vibrations to the fluid in the inner ear. The fluid then vibrates hair cells. These vibrations activate brain cells. Finally, the brain turns the vibrations into sounds. There are two types of deafness. Conduction deafness is a blocking of sound waves to the inner ear. An example is too much ear wax. Nerve deafness is when cells in the ear are damaged. Sound waves can't move from the inner ear to the brain. An example is children who are born deaf. Their middle or inner ear may be damaged.

The last sound Bell heard was his wife's voice. His wife said, "Don't leave me." Bell said, "No …" He died on August 2, 1922.

To honor his life, every phone in North America was silenced. This happened on August 4. Fourteen million phones were shut down for one minute. This happened at the exact moment Bell's body was put into the ground. Over 60,000 telephone operators stood silently. They didn't connect any calls.

Bell is honored in the science of sound. The standard unit for the intensity of sound waves is the "bel."

Mabel Bell died 5 months after Bell.

Timeline

1847: Bell was born. He was born in Edinburgh, Scotland. Edinburgh was known as the "Athens of the North." It has long been famous for its art, ideas, and inventions.

1859: Bell made his first invention. He made a machine that could clean wheat grains.

1870: Bell's brother, Melville, died. Bell moved to Canada with his family. The new climate made him healthier.

1871: Bell moved to the United States. He lived in Boston, Massachusetts.

1872: Bell opened up a school for the deaf. Helen Keller was one of his students.

1873: Bell became a professor at Boston University. He met Mabel Hubbard. Hubbard was a deaf student. Bell tutored her.

1874: Bell invented the telephone. He continued to work on it.

1877: Bell married Hubbard. They went to London for a year.

1878: Bell showed the telephone to Queen Victoria.

1881: President Garfield was shot. Bell tried to find the bullet. He used his x-ray machine invention. He couldn't find it.

1897: Bell became president of the National Geographic Society. His daughter had married the editor. His family members are still involved in this society today.

1915: Bell called Watson on the first transcontinental call. He called from New York. Watson was in San Francisco.

1922: Bell died. He's buried at Beinn Bhreagh in Canada. This is the summer home Bell built. It reminded him of his birthplace.

Consider This!

Take a Position! Research Elisha Gray. Some people think Gray may have invented the telephone first. What do you think? Argue your point with reasons and evidence.

Say What? Read the 45th Parallel Press book about Albert Einstein. Compare Einstein to Bell. Explain how they're alike. Explain how they're different.

Think About It! How often do you use the phone? What other inventions do we have today because of the phone? What would life be like without phones? Make a list of how your life would be different.

Learn More

Bader, Bonnie. *Who Was Alexander Graham Bell?* New York: Grosset & Dunlap, 2013.

Carson, Mary Kay. *Alexander Graham Bell for Kids: His Life and Inventions, with 21 Activities.* Chicago: Chicago Review Press, 2018.

Fraser, Mary Ann. *Alexander Graham Bell Answers the Call.* Watertown, MA: Charlesbridge, 2017.

Matthews, Tom L. *Always Inventing: A Photobiography of Alexander Graham Bell.* Washington, DC: National Geographic Children's Books, 2015.

Glossary

automaton (aw-TOM-uh-ton) moving machines that copy humans and are lifelike; robots

barbarous (BAHR-ber-uhs) cruel

deaf (DEF) unable to hear

experiment (ik-SPER-uh-ment) to test, to play around

manual (MAN-yoo-uhl) done with the hands

patents (PAT-uhnts) special ownership rights given to inventors to prevent people from stealing their ideas

pitch (PICH) the degree of highness or lowness of a tone

vibrations (vye-BRAY-shuhnz) back and forth motions

Index

aviation, 13

Bell, Alexander Graham, 4
    death of, 29
    education, 22–23
    experiments, 18, 20
    family, 6, 9, 11
    invents telephone, 4, 19, 21, 29
    middle name, 6, 9
    mother, 6, 10, 12, 14
    other inventions, 22, 25, 26
    patents, 4
    as pianist, 14–15, 17
    studies sound, 17, 20, 25, 29
    talking dog, 18, 20
    and telephone operators, 16, 29
    timeline, 30
    wife, 10, 13, 29
Bell Telephone Company, 5

deafness, 4, 10, 12, 13, 20, 25, 28

Gray, Elisha, 21

hearing aid, 10

lipreading, 13

manual alphabet, 12

Nutt sisters, 16

sound, 17, 20, 25, 28, 29

talking dog, 18, 20
telephone, 4, 19, 21, 29
telephone operators, 16, 29

Watson, Thomas, 4
women, 13, 16

About the Author

Dr. Virginia Loh-Hagan is an author, university professor, and former classroom teacher. She uses the phone all the time. She likes to talk a lot. She lives in San Diego with her very tall husband and very naughty dogs. To learn more about her, visit www.virginialoh.com.